INSPECTOR INSPECTOR

Jee Leong Koh is the author of *Steep Tea* (Carcanet), named a Best Book of the Year by the *Financial Times* and a Finalist by Lambda Literary in the United States. He has published four other books of poems, a volume of essays, a collection of zuihitsu, and a hybrid work of fiction titled *Snow at 5 PM: Translations of an Insignificant Japanese Poet*. *Inspector Inspector* is his second Carcanet book. Born and raised in Singapore, educated in England, Koh lives in New York City, where he heads the literary non-profit Singapore Unbound.

INSPECTOR
INSPECTOR

JEE LEONG KOH

CARCANET POETRY

First published in Great Britain in 2022 by
Carcanet
Alliance House, 30 Cross Street
Manchester, M2 7AQ
www.carcanet.co.uk

ISBN 978 1 80017 222 7

Book design by Andrew Latimer
Printed in Great Britain by SRP Ltd, Exeter, Devon

The publisher acknowledges financial
assistance from Arts Council England.

CONTENTS

In memory of
KOH DUT SAY
(1937–2018)

PALINODE IN THE VOICE OF MY DEAD FATHER (1)

Your mom, look
at her, crying

so piteously,
as my body is

wheeled
into the fire.

There she goes,
collapsing

into herself,
like a burning roof.

Hold her up.
Hold her

close, my
Hecuba.

I'm sorry I
ever thought

of her
as Helen.

PALINODE IN THE VOICE OF MY DEAD FATHER (II)

Tell your mom
I don't

love her less
than your sister.

I didn't
speak to my wife

last because
we had

a whole life
together.

I thought
it was fair

since she has
our vows

your sister
has her dad's

last words.
I'm full,

I nodded to
the bowl

of pork porridge
she brought.

If I had
to do it again,

I would have done it
differently,

but there's no
do again

when one is dead
and now

your mom
is always hungry.

PALINODE IN THE VOICE OF MY DEAD FATHER (III)

All the time
the air sacs

in my lungs
winked out

like lights
in an inhabited

valley,
the locks

of my heart
closed

at semi-regular
intervals,

my legs
waterlogged,

I thought,
I have no regrets

for living
the way I did, where I did.

The lights
blessed

the smoky Saturday dances
with the

implausibly
slim waists

of girls.
The canals met

us with boats
on their leisured

way
somewhere

to which our legs
would deliver us.

But we never
left the valley.

We bought a house,
paid for

by running
the machines maintaining

cool and comfortable
the valley air.

We had the two
of you,

as the valley said
to do.

And then, first,
the smog drifted

over
from the next valley

and choked to death
all our animals

and the smog,
staying years and years,

so long we had almost
acclimatized ourselves to it,

was followed
by the flood.

Likelihood

Remembering Lee Kuan Yew (1923–2015)

Like you, I went to Raffles Institution. Like you,
I joined the scouts to be rugged and played chess.
Unlike you, I was not the top student of Malaya,
nowhere near, but like you I got out with the cash.

My university studies were, like yours, delayed,
not by the violations of war, but by NS,
and so I learned to kowtow to the world. Like you,
I was educated in England but in The Other Place.

Like you, grasping the powerful grip of unity,
I acquired a long-lasting taste for independence.
Unlike you, I did not found a political party,
found another party for hot and heavy action.

While you were building a society, I built a school.
Like you, I did not tolerate dissent, my boss said
in an evaluation that was Catherine Lim's equal.
Like you, I have evolving views. Like you, I wept.

Like you, I am a writer. Unlike you, I write poems.
You wrote about your struggle learning Chinese;
I wrote about my struggle learning American;
foreigners riffing on affordable necessities.

Like it or not, I'm more like you than I'm like Mao,
Mahatma Gandhi, Mahathir, Major, or Madison.
Less like the Ghost than we are like the Holy Goh,
you are much more like me than God is like his Son.

Jogging in front of me in Central Park is a man,
a head all whitened, like a public man half naked.
What *is* the likelihood that he's you? In my mind,
I am, like you, very likely a moving target.

Gaudy Boy

*'afflicted with joy' – Arthur Yap, 'gaudy turnout', written during his year
in Leeds, UK*

Because you smell good. Because you spell éclat
as tear to pieces. Because gaudy means originally
delightful, as in annual college feasts (*British*),
the largest ornamental bead in a rosary, a jest.

Or else it means a yellow dye from dyer's rocket.
Because in your turnout, one cold night in Leeds,
Arthur pricks you out and in the moon's half-light
in fear of the ear of night and of the eye of day,

but mostly of the cellar of your heart, coal scuttle,
and we who think we are in the clear, fiercely free
of prayer, smell, and fear, we who justify ourselves,
dare to take pity on you, soluble crossword puzzle,

we read the *Times* and Arthur in parti-colored dress
and o yes, o well, the joke has always been on us.

Viewing Martin Ramírez at the American Folk Art Museum
after a Night of Fucking in a Lycra Suit

(after Yeow Kai Chai)

in anhedonia	i hide an anon
catatonic dreams	mace c-data on stir
of kittens in ovens	o tens of tin knives
alogia wilderness	loading a wireless
spandex	expands
the jerk chickun	the Jurchen kick
genetically mute	met in glutey lace
the lucky allele	all they eke and cull
not martin ramírez	nor trim ez martian
pregnancy stress or	cypresses n grantor
cannabis use	e-scan a bi-sun
committed 'im	mode mic mitt
to institutions	on its tot in situ
and also art	raton as lad

Squatting Quietly

for Cyril Wong

He was tall and skinny. Boyish face. Thin hair. He was seven years younger than I but he seemed older, not just touched by experience, but scarred. His book of poems bore witness to the wounds. Probed the wounds of family and love with such lyrical honesty that I was transfixed in the Times Bookshop where I picked up the slim volume. The book was called *Squatting Quietly*. In Singapore, people squatted in toilets to shit. Ah Bengs, young toughs, squatted on sidewalks outside shopping centers, puffed their cigarettes, cursed in Hokkien and teased the girls strolling by. As I stared from the back of the café at Cyril Wong reading, I thought I could detect the squat in his stance. It had something of defensiveness in it, as when one squats to make oneself a smaller target. But it had a greater measure of defiance.

Conciliatory by temperament, I was drawn to this public display of shamelessness. In the months after the reading, we went out for coffee a couple of times and I plied him with questions about writing. He was the published poet, I was the wannabe. We talked about his coming-out as gay to his family, his experience cruising for sex in public restrooms, his opinions of other poets. Hiding behind these questions, I came close each meeting to telling him that I too was gay, that I didn't have a clue what to do about it. It must have been obvious to him, but he didn't hurry me. He allowed me to tell him at my own time.

It was some years later, and half a world away, when I did. I had moved to New York, fallen in and out of love, started publishing. I sent Cyril a copy of my first book. He had been sending me his books, written with enviable regularity. Then one special volume came in the post one day. It wasn't published by his usual publisher, but by a press that he set up for the book. *Satori Blues* had a very pale yellow cover and wide French flaps. Inside was inscribed 'for Jee Leong, with love & respect'. I was pleased and flattered. By that time, however, I didn't want his respect for declaring myself gay; I wanted his respect for my writing. I wanted affirmation that, late starter that I was, I had caught up.

I read *Satori Blues* in a complicated spirit of rivalry and adoration. As if the poet and I were a couple looking for a threesome. If the reader flirted with him, I felt proud of my lover but disappointed for myself. Worse if the stud sweet-talked me, for I couldn't enjoy the attention, knowing that my lover was overlooked. The gay domestic trope wasn't irrelevant to the book. By that time, Cyril had happily settled down with his partner. My boyfriend and I had just moved in together. I was looking forward to a new phase of life and was casting about for a way to think about it.

Woven from Buddhist philosophies, *Satori Blues* provided, still provides, such a way. It is a way of joy. The poem traverses the terrains of pain, sorrow, pity, and outrage, but all 337 lines of it are suffused with joy, concentrating and dispersing in this epiphany:

> Light carves my shadow into a rock,
> beckons and merges it with the shadow
> of a tree. A child's laugh calls down
> bridges into this world. That slow walk
> back to the car, our minds filled with
> inaudible music.

The poem is cast in the form of a meditation, 'a stream of consciousness', says its blurb, but it is ultimately, I believe, a love song. 'This number is for you,' *Satori Blues* concludes. In this number, the squatting young man in the poet stands up. I climb to my feet too, for the poem asks me to 'sing along'.

Missing Subject Line

for Arthur Yap (1943–2006)

Elsa,

I've just received the package of bones you sent!
I've always wanted the complete set
to check if his throat cancer left a mark.

What fun to hold a familiar funny bone and hear
it speak again of a painted scroll,
I know the stupid bird can never eat the stupid peach,

and another, offal smooth, never seen before,
a pig is a very compact arrangement,
and wonder where it fits.

The bone for Keith
keeps its silence about a word –

charged with holding the courts in contempt,
the blogger Alex Au
argued the word is *gay,*

Cyril (remember him?), bless his heart,
believes it is *goodness,*
while I fancy *you* –

and so the linguist speaks eternally.

Ha, ha! Arthur Yap, I have your bones all in one place,
as others do who cherish completeness,
far from home, above the ground, and unquiet.

Thank you.

The Peace Lily

for Justin Chin (1969, Kuantan, Malaysia–2015, San Francisco, USA)

I will sit here and think of Justin Chin.
Here is my laptop and the peace lily
I bought from Lloyd in the makeshift greenhouse,
the trains above making a muted racket.

Lloyd's Black but he reminded me of you.
It was the way he managed the street shop
without seeming to manage it. His eyes,
kingpins, did not nail down my back and bag.

The plants around seemed to speak for him,
boxwood, snake plant, and bird of paradise,
as he transferred the lily to the black ceramic
pot and dish I had picked out. No charge,
Lloyd added, eyes smiling, for repotting it.

One leaf turned yellow yesterday. Dammit.

To a Young Poet

Quit the country soon as you can
before you're set on a career path or marrying
the home ownership scheme.
Pay no heed to the village elders.
They are secretly ashamed that they did not leave.

Quit the country but do not
shake the dust off your feet against it.
Leave instead with a secret smile
for all that leaving has to teach you.

Learn what it is to be welcomed
for the coin in your purse, for strong hips
in pushing a cart uphill, a firm voice in a good cause.
When the welcome wears off, as it will,
learn to leave again, this time by the sea.

Be always on your way, and on arrival
sleep with anyone who asks. You never know
what gift they may have for you in the morning.
You will discover, suddenly or over the course of a winter night,
what gift you have for them.
Always kiss goodbye on the lips.

There will be seasons of great loneliness.
You cannot outrun it, so sit and survey
the thunderless desert.

In every town, pick up the local accent
and blend it into yours, already impure,
as a secret ingredient is fused into the top note of a perfume.
Hearing you, the taberna will wonder where you are from.
Drink deep of their wonderment. Do not betray it.

After you leave a good tip for the barkeep,
climb to your narrow room and write whatever you wish.
Your flowers will grace the sweaty brow of a buffalo.
Your politics will smell of perfume.
If you write about the old country, you will write
about a lover who leaves your side in the night
to stand by the window and look up at the crescent moon.

PALINODE IN THE VOICE OF MY DEAD FATHER (IV)

I met a suicide
here,

a young man
who looked

eighteen,
who could not

stop talking
in parables.

He had made
the world

a better place,
he was convinced,

by leaving it,
but, boy,

how he missed,
how he missed,

his friend
who was more than a friend.

PALINODE IN THE VOICE OF MY DEAD FATHER (V)

At the cinema
you were

excited by the bare-bodied
students

of kungfu
lifting water buckets

on their broad
shoulders,

the Hollywood
car chase

led by an amnesiac
Marine captain

at the flashing wheel,
and so was I,

looking for a shot
of testosterone

in
my disabled life,

until the picture
of you

taken from behind
came unbidden

on the screen,
and I

had to close my eyes
against

the fire engulfing
the overturned

car, the water buckets
clattering

down
the temple steps.

PALINODE IN THE VOICE OF MY DEAD FATHER (VI)

Inside the heavy
canvas bag,

all greasy, sealed
with motor oil,

my handy pliers,
flat nose, round nose,

and needle,
my screwdrivers

of many lengths
and heads,

my ball peen
hammer,

the use of which
you never learned,

except
the measuring tape

I caught you
once

bandaging round
your biceps

and then
your unconcealed thighs.

PALINODE IN THE VOICE OF MY DEAD FATHER (VII)

The war
accommodated

me to hardship –
rooting

for a sweet potato
in a ditch,

flying
from the soldiers –

as much
as the prosperity afterwards

accommodated
you to success.

You escaped
the draft

for nation building
and wrote

your poetry
books.

Much as I wished
to do likewise,

throw down
the weight of duty,

like a sack
of rice,

I could not
run away

from the sweet potato
I had eaten.

from 'UNGOVERNABLE BODIES'

Carlos, November 30, 2006 (Thu), met again at Splash Bar, back in my place, 69, frottage.

A bedroom is not a bedroom unless it has
a means of egress, say the rules for sellers.
After the larks have sung, our Romeo must
have a system for leaving safely and secretly.

It is only after marrying that our lovers find,
at one tragic finish, one another in a tomb.
A bedroom is not a bedroom unless it has
a means of egress, say the rules for buyers.

Outside my room in Queens, a fire escape
for lovers who found their way to my bed.
Staring at its black, complicated extensions,

I wrote my earliest American poems about
freedom and happiness, misery and desire,
the night train frothing on the nearby track.

Andy, April 7, 2007 (Sat), met at Splash
Came back to my place. Mutual jerk off after I sucked him. He
does not suck or allow himself to be fucked. Likes cuddling in
bed.

He would not accept in any part of him,
neither his mouth nor arse, not his ears,
any protruding part belonging to a man,
not the cock, neither finger, toe, nor tongue,

as if, smooth as a pebble washed by the sea,
he was inviolable too, like the seaside stone,
as if to be smooth was to be unbroken
on any and all sides, round as infinity.

But he would allow his whole to be held,
the whole in a part or the part of a whole,
by the hand of a body or the body of a hand,

and taken up by a boyish choice and glee,
aimed with the slant of an eye, and flung –
a planet skipping into the ether of the sea.

Antonio, May 16, 2007 (Wed), my place
About to incorporate his real estate LLC. He talked about
spending a weekend together in Montauk. He kissed and bit
my butt and back of legs and rimmed me before rubbing his
dick between my thighs. Both of us wanted him to fuck me but
I stopped him because he had no condom. I jerked off while he
sucked my nipple.

Now 51 and fucking all the boys
on screen and nowhere else, in the half hour
before showering for work, no other time,
sucking in a paunch, straightening the back

when I pass by a mirror or a gorgeous man,
I curse myself for stopping you, Antonio,
from wreaking sweet destruction on my arse,
because neither of us owned a condom.

We took the train for the three-hour ride,
taking in every little station on Long Island,
sensing the ocean when we could not see it,

and just before the train pulled into Montauk
for the weekend binge-eating and sunbathing,
I jumped off – yes, it was just like that.

Andy, May 27, 2007 (Sun), Mr. Black
Andy came back to my place. Arousing to suck him and then to
jerk off myself. He stayed until Monday afternoon.

The tunnel has been closed for some time now,
but a claw of panthers find their cast-iron steps
from daylight street to basement dungeon
to suffer the flail of ecstasy. Mr Conductor,

when will train service begin, the velvet
rope that ties one to all harmonically?
The Rose Boy is antsy. The brick arches
jump from toe to toe, making an entrance

for the Black Detective with a blank map.
He does not come in the name of the law,
but with a nose ring that glints in the dark.

Follow him! Father has been buried here
for far too long. We will exhume his bones
and beat a retreat playfully with the femur.

after Yeow Kai Chai

Andy, June 16, 2007 (Sat), my sister's place in Fairfax County, Virginia
Phone sex. Mutual jerk off.

It's not a design flaw, but a design plus,
the weak digital signal from my phone
to the equally weak receiver in yours,
the call boosted by the tall radio mast,

for our heated talk cannot be stopped
and it cannot stop another's intercourse
as long as we are all on frequencies
slightly different, long undulating waves.

The all-important mast cannot be marriage,
although I'm calling from the home office
in my dear sister's three-bedroom house,

but multiple coordinated arrangements
for long-term care and instant kindness,
in radio cells of the give of honeycomb.

Mike, June 22, 2007 (Fri), Urge Bar, then my place
Mother half-black & half-Irish, Father half-Scottish & half-
Irish. Light-skinned, cute face, with ear studs, plump, hairy
chest and groin but not overly so, uncut. Blowjobs and then he
fucked me, and nearly brought me to the edge. Nice guy, good
conversationalist.

Half-time. Hyphenated adjectives.
Hefted to the edge. Holy shit!
Half-boiled eggs. High and low.
Ho, ho, ho, the phone clock rhymes.

Borderlands half-awake. Hot takes
on a hairy chest but not overly so.
History. Handfuls of old chestnuts.
Half-Black, half-Irish, half-Scottish.

Hackers of the world, unite haply!
Hundreds of centaurs and unicorns,
wholesome as Angel, hip as River.

Half-life only is my life, haiku-like,
compromised, lukewarm, judas,
but, hey, I'm uncut too, hallelujah!

Andy, July 1, 2007 (Sun), my place
Came to my place and we had sex. Took Monday off from work
and walked in Central Park and had dinner in Chelsea.

The day after sex should be a day off
for contemplation, walking in the park,
or basically doing nothing at all,
except to reunite the shattered body.

Here comes a leg floating down the river,
the left appendage judging by its toes.
Rescue the right hand, so helpful last night,
before it hunts and gathers yet again.

Now we wait for the torso, the exposed
and powerful chest, the hardworking abs,
the part that's made up of so many parts,

and following behind the skinny ass,
the daily deviser of good and evil,
bobbing like an apple the singing head.

PALINODE IN THE VOICE OF MY DEAD FATHER (VIII)

Yes, the Prime Minister
is here too,

in this day-night.
He sits

on a rocky outcrop,
silent, unwilling

to retract
his expressed regret

for sending
women to college

and other
stubborn opinions.

When I asked
him about

his children's
fight over

his house, whether
it should be

torn down or turned
into a museum,,

he could not speak.
He had tears

in his eyes but no tongue
in his mouth.

He has made his will
and will swear by it.

PALINODE IN THE VOICE OF MY DEAD FATHER (IX)

Remember that construction
worker

run over
by the bus, setting off

a riot?
I see him

in every Indian here,
short or tall,

handsome
or devastated,

starving or sleek-headed
and satisfied.

I can't help it.
Why can't I

see Rajaratnam
our Deputy

Prime Minister or
the guitarist Alex

Abisheganaden instead?
I go up,

like getting on
a bus,

to every Indian here
and I ask,

are you
Sakthivel Kumaravelu?

And they say,
every one

of them, smiling,
or grimacing, or

furrowing
the brow,

Don't you wish
for me to be him?

from 'A SIMPLE HISTORY OF SINGAPOREANS IN AMERICA'

The Ceramicist

for Hong-Ling Wee (arr. 1992)

On a NASA scholarship to map the world,
she walked into a workshop on a whim
to throw a lump of clay on a wheel and feel
a foggy, quiet, pink, revolving world
evolve into an object of the mind
under the body's pressure, slight and sure,
and, afterwards, surrender to the fire,
not that of fire, but that of accident,
for a ceramic rocket fallen back
to earth. And this she did, for many years,
living on little, explaining less, until
she was surrounded by the fuselage.
When the towers gashed vermilion and buckled,
she was alone at home in Union Square.
The noise expanded as it dribbled off
to meet its echo, second detonation
worse than the first report, in summoning
half-buried images of Hiroshima
and Nagasaki. In a foreign mood,
she heard the phone ring and a female voice,
acclimatized but recognizable
as Singaporean, asked for Wee Hong Ling.
She never tires of telling this story, how
the Consulate located her and every
Singaporean within an hour of disaster,

when a black hole opened but was avoided
because a star had called, a star called home.
She never tires of telling this story, which
I now tell you in my own fanciful way,
each iteration also explanation,
the how developing into the why,
why her pitchers, bowls, vases levitate.

The Columnist

for Kopin Tan, who renounced his Singapore citizenship in October, 2018.

The questionnaire required him to rank
his top three reasons. Children's education.
Property prices. NS. CPF.
Thinking the answers only acronyms
for the good life defined by Singapore,
he chose to write next to the label Others.
He could have said he was the very first
gay Asian columnist for Barron's, with
tens of thousands of followers, death threats
for dumping on the casinos, and he
threw over the stock market for his novel.
Or, more facetiously, he could have said
he liked Tate's cookies. Or, more tellingly,
the pictures of his SG friends and wives,
but when he posted on Facebook holiday
snaps of his husband, deafening silence.
They liked his cheesecake photos well enough.
They did not like the pics of Tom and him.
Being an aspiring writer, he could have
added the grace note of that special time,
his teens, nose in *The Swimming Pool Library*,
he read about sex in the changing room,
another swimming pool in an elite school
floated to mind, also the swimming trunks
suspended at the back of the classroom
to dry (hearing him speak, I saw again
the wing-cowering, petroleum-covered birds),
what made the younger female teachers blush.
The trunks spoke volumes: he the willing scribe

could just outline their bios in this form,
enough to rub some noses in the pubes.
Or else he could have added, for the record,
before reason number one, before zero,
he was a block away from World Trade Center,
doing an interview with some big shot,
in Marriot's Room 1703,
when the first tower chased a falling man
down to the ground, and everything the dust
covered turned white. Sprinting down, he was
out on the street to cover the event,
following his reporter's nose. Bodies,
or what could be identified as bodies,
leeched the lifeblood from his face. Strangers stripped
their dress shirts off for masks and doused them
from bottles given free by hotdog vendors.
The smoldering smell persisted on Wall Street
more than a month later. Once in a while
the subway car would hear a cry, and sob.
He bonded with his city then, I thought,
reading his article, a hymn of love,
a declaration, a new constitution
drawn up, and ratified by meeting Tom
in Therapy, the bar and not the shrink,
and marrying in New York's City Hall.
He could have said, gaily, and that is why
I'm turning in my passport and IC,
one long expired, but the other not,
and what he declared would have been a lie.
It would not have taken into account
the sad little bar squatting at the top
of Lucky Plaza, where men fell each night
into their drinks and could no way be dried.
The lonely hours of driving in a shell,

where was no standing up or lying down
but offered escape still, no questions asked
but Whitney's 'Don't you wanna dance with me'
on Nicoll Drive, which ran beside the coast
but wrote and rewrote O, number and letter.
Because of those drowned mouths, he was to write
for his one reason on the questionnaire
the criminalization of homo...
quantified those hours as 377
and graded his own answer with an A.

The Author

for Kevin Kwan, who moved to Houston, Texas, at the age of 11

No fences. Cool. No sentry boxes. Cool,
the driveway stripes, the handkerchief-neat lawns,
like in the movies, *Home Alone,* or something.
He was not so hot about no maids. Lunch box
he had to pack himself and find his way
not only to but through Clear Lake High School,
the normal life his father engineered,
far away from hereditary privilege.
Who would anticipate the terminus,
the cancer in the family that struck
by lottery, and made him drop New York
for an uncertain term by his father's bed?
There they turned over still-bright memories
of Singapore, the gate that always squeaked,
the taste of Newton wanton mee, the click
of mahjong tiles, the garden birthday parties,
and shared a joke or else a thought, a word
or three, like crazy rich Asians. And yet
another privilege – the clean, white pillow
grew hot under father and he flipped it
for a cool offertory to the head.
I know he did. Last year I did the same.

The Muslim

for Zizi Azah Abdul Majid (Ourika Café, Lower East Side, NYC,
January 6, 2019)

In the soft, low hurry of her voice I
hear why she named her daughter Zinira,
after the Roman slave so savagely
tortured for her new faith, her only God,
a scarf tightened around and in her eyes.
She was at Trader Joe's and kneeling down
for Zini's vitamins on the bottom shelf
when a Black woman cried in a loud voice,
'Why are you praying here? Stop your praying.
This is America.' Once, at Columbia,
a play about the siege of Leningrad
was read in a workshop. Shocked by the news,
she asked the playwright, 'Is it true, they boiled
their dead and ate the soup?' Overhearing her,
the actor, a white graduate student, smiled:
'What do you think? Those halal carts, who knows
what they put in to make the food taste good!'
The joke blindsided her. She can't forget,
standing with Zini by their car, outside
the supermarket in Connecticut,
a Jewish man wearing a Jewish hat
espying her tudung, accosted her
for her opinion on the Middle East,
the bombing of the bus in Jerusalem,
his face so close she only saw his eyes.
She took her own sweet time to go to God.
After her heart stopped in the hospital,
her grandmother woke up from her coma
a vegetative thing, dear thing, and lived

with Zizi's family for four years. Her uncle,
who went to Pearl Jam concerts with his wife
and cheered on her choice to wear the burka,
was thrown off from his motorbike and died.
She closed her show in Singapore and drove
to sit in KL with sequestered grief.
Along the drive up north and afterwards,
the question, like a supertitle, flashed –
'Why do I have to wait for someone else
to die before I take faith seriously?'
She started by praying five times a day,
pulled on long sleeves and then pulled on long pants,
smiled, frowned, smirked, narrowed her eyes at the mirror
before she ventured out, her hair well hidden.
It helped that Izmir gave her for her birthday
an Alexander McQueen headscarf, all
grinning skulls and smoky purple and brown.
She tells me this because she believes faith
is modern and because she knows I think
it's hip, a silky crown by another queen,
and will include the detail in my poem,
and so I do. She's writing a play now
about a rock band from Syria, whose faith
in music is contested by the war,
her graduate thesis on grudging theisms.
She loves New York. And Zini loves it too.
In school she studies French and Mandarin,
besides English; ethics and art as well.
She reads her storybooks when out of school,
and weaves her tapestry and plays the piano,
and when she is not doing any of these,
she writes poems. She will learn soon enough
whom she is writing for, beyond herself,
her separate and united audiences,

who grow clearer when she closes her eyes,
as her namesake praised God for blinding her
and for returning her sight praised Him again.

The Art Director

for Mark Yeo (Madam Zhu's Kitchen, West Village, NYC, October 24, 2019)

Not knowing the West Village was Manhattan,
for months the naif longed to see Manhattan.
The fucking bimbo! If Abby threw him out,
his plan was to bus tables and live in the Bronx
under the railway tracks. Always exploring
he was, meeting the crazies and the druggies
in Williamsburg, running home from the bus,
terrified of being mugged or worse. Ten dollars
his daily budget – thank you, Chinese takeouts –
and once he busted it on *Mission Impossible*.
But he knew, *knew*, he was in the right place.
The parties, for one, where his habiliment,
once a headgear topped by a cymbal-clapping
wind-up monkey for a Moroccan party,
never let down his hosts, attracting chatter,
shutters, and eyelash flutters. For another,
after 10 letters a day and cold calling,
the job offers came in with a green card.
(They loved his light box of a portfolio.)
For yet another, the boy would have died
in Singapore, according to the doctors
who blamed the weather for mystery sicknesses,
and there were signs, so many fucking signs,
not in the stars, but in *Star Wars*, big things
awaiting the foolhardy, the resistance,
who scored A's in all subjects but F9
in Engrish; who were the last families
to leave their old kampong in Yio Chu Kang,
hating the Death Star of a HDB block,
and, sure enough, the mutt Ah Fat next day

died of heartbreak; who were protected by
a gui ren, the Jedi of a dead grandfather,
until they learned to stand up for themselves
and say, I speak slowly only for your sake.
If you don't understand my accent, ah,
I feel sorry for you but I wun change.
According to my family, it's our fate
to be together in this life and place,
so live the max and make the best of it
for once. For we will never meet again.

The Speculative Fiction Writer

for Manish Melwani (Rasa Malaysian Restaurant, West Village, NYC, March 25, 2019)

Would Partition had not birthed two babies,
one named what was, the other what could be,
because the family had then found itself
torn in two, between staying and going,
and followed finally the Sindhi way,
teleporting all to Morocco, Burma,
and, in his Dada's case, to Singapore.
Would he, Manish Melwani, at his Maths
had scored and had not been turfed (luckily!)
from Anglo-Chinese to American,
where Mr. Silverman showed him the art
of penning science fiction, of building worlds,
man-eating flowers, fantastic egg-shaped mounds,
nor taken on the rap of gangsta chic,
under the influence of Wu Tang Clan,
and drunk on weekends with the sonabitches
who never gave him time of day but now
hung out with him, guardian of the gateway
to girls, the jagar of their Shangri-la,
because out of despair's hairy armpit
he rode the winged creature, confidence,
to summer school at the Jack Kerouac
and worked with Chip, who tore apart his novel
but recommended him to Clarion.
There, the unreal encounter with real friends
and the embodiment of love. The call,
there, to drop advertising for authorship,
copywriting for writing. There. Would Wells,
Clarke, Asimov and the other grandmasters

had breathed diversity into their aliens,
would Herbert had not modeled Arakkis
on Iraq, because the alien trope exerted
a stranglehold on our imagination.
Speculations flower from the soil of facts.
They become facts. Back home in Singapore,
the Aljunieds, the great trading Yemenis,
who lived in Malaya even before Raffles,
are quizzed about where they come from, as if
only the Chinese are Singaporeans.
Tharman, the best person to lead the country,
is declared unelectable because
Singapore is not ready for an Indian
Prime Minister, for such an oxymoron.
It is enough to turn anyone's head
egg-white with grief or to a raging pyre.
The casual slurs – man, can't you take a joke –
downed at house parties with a whiskey neat,
the house plants baring their titanium teeth.
Entering NS with the Poly batch,
he left the champagne Bubble when he met
Punjabi boys whose fathers drove the taxis
he liked to imagine as time machines,
whose mothers cleaned the hospitals, the boys
already men in trials of wit and strength.
His gray Enciks, who happened to be Sikhs,
warned him against joining the army – he
would hentak kaki as a captain forever
while junior officers, some whom he trained,
who happened to be Chinese, got promoted.
Two worlds. Three. Four. He was in Singapore
when Sakthivel Kumaravelu died
under the wheels of a bus on Race Course Road
and fellow workers, most from Tamil Nadu,

smashed the offensive vehicle that whisked
them out of sight to tight and spartan dorms,
overturned police cars, set them on fire,
threw bottles, rocks, eggplants, at Special Ops.
He was the men who struck the ambulance
and also was the men in yellow vests
who stumbled out of it, hands shielding heads,
making a desperate run for safety. Would
Sinnathamby Rajaratnam, sometimes
he had thought while composing in New York
his paper on the Third World for the panel
at the 3rd SLF, would the Deputy
Prime Minister had stayed a fiction writer
in London, a writer noticed by George Orwell,
a writer with a deep love for the poor,
a writer who would have imagined him,
instead of turning his pen hand to power,
bringing a nation, not a novel, to
Being. Reality. Would he. Would he.

The Daughter

for Marguerita Choy (Barawine, Harlem, December 10, 2018)

They had always had animals at home,
welcoming every stray, kittens and pups,
into the house on Jalan Emas Urai,
the kinder of the neighbors named The Shelter.
Better god's creatures than the devil's beasts.
Her father grew up in occupied Ipoh
and, to help his family, sold vegetables
under the noses of the Japanese.
Her mother was an Austrian who did not
care for the Germans. The Americans
neither when their planes strafed a passenger train.
They met in London, after World War II,
he a law student and she an au pair,
and made a family home of Singapore.
Now they live in the city of Dundee,
where she and her sister had gone to school,
and where the older stayed to doctor fate
and bring up her own alien family.
A link, a leash, tenuous and Scottish.
Her mother now alone in a nursing home,
a fact her father forgets when he wanders
beyond the confines of his house to search
for missing animals. The year's been hard,
hardly a golden year. Right in New York,
Reuters is cutting staff into the bone.
Her cat has sprung a fang and it looks bad.
This Christmas, she will leave with Clay and Mag
the ailing pet and with the ailing parents
spend what little time she had to spare
from her preoccupation with Lafayette.

The Porn Star

for Annabel Chong (fl. 1994–2003)

Who killed Annabel Chong, I hear you ask.
Her mother, when she tied the babysitter,
a handkerchief, to the kindergartner's front
to swipe away her where-is-mummy tears.
The trauma, opined the female critic, emptied
Annabel for all the dicks in her porn career.
That's why the porn star wished in self-delusion
to make her parents proud, as mum was proud
her daughter rubbed the faces of her friends,
crying their hearts out, with the stitch of fabric.
She was an overachiever, a gifted kid,
and like so many of her 80's cohort
killed off her inhibitions once abroad.
Half-drunk, one night, alone, in London town,
she followed off the train a smiling man.
(Me too, late in the naughts, right off the PATH
into a cozy home in Hoboken.
He came, I had not, but was ushered out
into the empty city. To this day,
I still remember the Munch reproductions.)
The Brit raped her and in the unlit alley
appeared his lads, from god knows where, and had
their turn, orderly as at a lunch counter.
Did she die then? Was it a ghost of vengeance
who flew to L.A. and filmed with football jocks
'I Can't Believe I Did the Whole Team',
flanked by the furies of two Asian sisters?
L.A., Hugh Hefner's playground and capital.
If Armageddon hit the world, she thought
in movie terms, it would begin in L.A..

Cupped in the hills above Hollywood,
the sets of an engorged porn industry,
the disused warehouses and private homes
through which the touted milk of human kindness –
directors, actors, and crewmembers – spurted.
Here Annabel met John T. Bone and made
her mark, bossed by the man from Manchester.
'The World's Biggest Gangbang' shot her to fame.
A porno arms race, post-Cold War, took off –
who could shoot more, buy more, sell more, take more.
Billed as 300 men, really 70,
all shapes and sizes, colors, looks, and ages,
committed 251
sex acts with the porn star Annabel Chong.
Unknown to her, not all of them were tested
for HIV, not all attested clean.
Between a colonnade of phalluses,
fake Doric columns, plaster Venuses
in various states of undress interspersed,
a garden worthy of a Messalina
in Hollywood, the would-be lovers snaked
and, five at a time, mounted the platform,
blue with a polyester tarp, and tupped
the self-identifying 'female stud'.
Mr T. Bone, at a water break, asked her,
'Annabel, what makes you such a sexual monster?'
He never paid her although he made a killing.
He did not kill her. She tested negative
and after acting and directing some,
including the gangbang film *Pornomancer*,
her take on William Gibson's novel, she
got fucking bored of fucking with Annabel.
She took a job in IT, announced it
the vile work of the Evil Doppelgänger.

Uncannily, refusing to be canned,
Annabel Chong was primed for resurrection
by heroin addict and mommy's boy
Gough Lewis, whose doco on Annabel
provided some material for this poem.
He never got 'The World's' a parody,
a para-ode, beside the fucking point.
I quote from a late interview she gave:
'Sometimes I'd be talking about sex,'
Annabel said, 'in a more philosophical
way and he wouldn't really understand.'
How then could such a man edit her ideas
when she had always done the cutting herself?
One of the film producers Suzanne Whitten
renamed the film 'Sex: the Gough Lewis Story
told by Gough Lewis through Annabel Chong'.
The gaffe by Gough. You see the irony?
The subject turns out to be the subject,
even from the beginning of the world,
the Word with God, was God, and all that jizz.
One man at the big bang was trying to get
into the business. Another, from New York,
was there for the adventure. The third wanted
to be a part of history. Middle-aged
and balding, the fourth man on camera
was holding a red rose in a plastic sheath.
All left me just looking. A ragged bloom
I raised, unbidden, when a cute young blond
kneeled down to eat her cunt as the Empress,
deathless as digital storage, one and zero,
clumsily removed her gold lamé dress.

The Prodigal

for Justin Chin (1969, Kuantan, Malaysia–2015, San Francisco, USA)

He took his fortune on the road – a toke
of toxic stories, like the moths in May
so easily swatted into pure asbestos.
Hawaii was the first stop but SF
beckoned with its buff fags and druggy poets,
Tom Sellecks into golden showers while
reciting Les Fleurs du fucking mal.
To use the body up, disintegrate
into the yellow shards of the forsythia,
to savor the next day the rally, slow
and painstaking, of muscle, bone, and blood
in morning muck and in the sty of style
was well worth living for, dying for, even.
How proud he was, the prodigal, when he
hit upon making the mom watch her son,
she hazy with Alzheimer's, he with coke,
receive the shit unreeling from his trick
into his mouth, like a communion wafer,
while she disposes, satchel after satchel,
sugar into hers, scattering stray crystals
onto her front, transforming her housedress
into the sequined gown of a drag queen.
There is no turning point in Justin's story,
no moment when the son came to his senses
(he was already living through his senses),
not even when he got his diagnosis.
Just this: you're watching TV with your dad,
about the water parks in the Middle East,
and the man makes a mess due to his meds.
When he gets up quietly, without a word,

to change his clothes and find the air freshener,
you look ahead, you do not turn your head,
at the fun waterslide, long as a mile,
with jets so powerful they can propel
a half-pint up and back from where he came.

The Father

for W. (Chengdu House, Chelsea, NYC, March 6, 2019)

What was compassion he learned when he helped
his older son fill up his college forms.
He wasn't so neglected his abuela
had to report to Children's Services.
He didn't grow up in a foster home.
He hadn't, every season, to meet strangers,
before he graduated out the system,
to play basketball, to make them like him,
afraid the whole time they would make him choose
between a real home and his younger brother,
or su hermano would choose home over him.
What would Admissions think of his expulsion
from school for selling his classmates his meds?
What of the second time he had to leave,
this time from boarding school, in the same year
as Trump's election? Rapists, criminals,
the President labeled all immigrants.
Not long ago the same slander applied
to men who lived with men and wanted sons.
In Singapore, the technocrat's wet dream,
he chose and was, it seemed, chosen, by merit.
Coming from no-name school to RJC,
he thought the students smug. Instead of joining
Humanities, he chose Arts stream to root
for local faculty. Instead of the Ivies,
he studied fashion at Parsons. Instead of
the Chelsea boy, he dated older men,
much older men, with stories of surviving
conversion therapy, gay bashing, AIDS,
heroic stories of protest and care.

He met his husband on Craigslist. He googled
the value of his home to judge it safe,
as he had always done. He didn't know
about the shootings in the neighborhood.
So much for Singapore-style planning! How
could he imagine in one year he would
marry in February, graduate in May,
and in June have the boys move in with them?
He had always been good at being trained
and the adoption training was not hard,
good at filling up forms, following rules,
at cost-and-benefit analysis,
but he had to be taught again and again,
by Christmas cacti as well as the boys,
their shooting, flourishing, yet homely needs
informing his attention, the feeling of
fear inalienable from fatherhood.

PALINODE IN THE VOICE OF MY DEAD FATHER (X)

I couldn't believe
my ashes

were lowered
by a

ribbon
into the sea

in a gift
box.

Not a chance
to stay

on anyone's
fingers.

Not a chance
to fly with the wind

and whip
back

into anyone's
eyes.

Singapore
does not take, nor give, chances.

You dropped me
off the

dedicated boat,
steered

by a Chinese man,
dark as a Malay,

to the
sea bed, where

I lay
unopened,

where I
thirstily dissolved.

The Goldfish Bowl

Supposedly a show of support for medical workers, the banging on pots and pans at exactly 5 pm every day is to scare off the demons. Listen to the hysteria detonating like Chinese firecrackers just beneath the grimness. You can hear it also on the liberal Internet. It has the sadness of dead goldfish floating to the top of the goldfish bowl, or bodies in body bags stacked into refrigerated trucks outside the hospital. Mask up, one health inspector says to another. I can't breathe, says the Black man locked down by a beast with six knees and hands. I should take to the streets, I say, but what if I catch the virus? I will write instead, in the privacy of 5 am, banging my pot against my pan in this way.

The Zoom Background

The missing person poster was sent to all households in the year of the Great Election. The picture was of my dead father. His face, racked with pain, became the most popular Zoom background, downloaded over a million times around the world. I wrote to the Internet safety bureau every day to ask them to scrub the web clean of the image. I did not wish to share my father with the world. In any case, he was not missing, he was dead. I saw his body pushed into the fire. I dropped his ashes into the sea. Finally, annoyed by my harassment, the Inspector General rained fingers on his keyboard and changed the poster from missing to wanted. The pain on my father's face then looked sinister. It was downloaded faster than ever, reaching a billion times in China alone.

The Cartoon Tavern

Cheap shots. Surgical strikes. Under the nose of the
elevator inspector, I have been drinking too much to
make up for missed drinks and dinners with friends,
book launches and readings, my 50th birthday celebration.
Extraordinary measures for extraordinary times. I have
been visiting the cartoon tavern run by Sir Meliodas, the
Dragon Sin of Wrath, to drink with all the other Sins. I
have been associating with a pig called Hawk. I have been
hell-bent to revive a dead fairy called Elaine. I have been
fighting an incredibly beautiful Holy Knight by the name
of Hendrickson, who has grown fantastically powerful by
ingesting demon blood. And after beating him down with
my Sacred Treasure, I have returned to the tavern and called
for another dram of druid fluid.

The Quaker Sunflower

Everyone on the show is paranoid, except for the Quaker,
who is plain creepy. I have located her creepiness in her
calm. While the detective inspectors are dashing all about
Dusseldorf, hunting down clues and connections, she
gardens at home, pausing to listen to your woes and dispense
wise advice. She is a friend to everyone. Her face is round
as a sunflower. She reminds me of a certain civil servant
in Singapore, met at a roundtable on arts diplomacy. After
flashing his PowerPoint slides at us, he took me aside to say
that he did not understand my unfriendliness towards the
National Arts Council. Surely it was better for everyone to
have their knives chained to the wall, and identified by QR
codes? He did not say this, but he could.

The Harlem Harem

I think I am collecting a harem of birds in Harlem. I am not
sure. I must be the most unsure Shah in Persian history. Some
days, the birds thrash in the luxurious appointments of my
head. Other days, the screechy gulls wheel away, each taking
a scrap of me in his beak, and barrel in so many different
directions that I despair of ever piecing myself back together,
even with the help of the inspector of public hygiene. I used
to pass by two elderly Black men in Marcus Garvey Park, who
scattered breadcrumbs to the pigeons, and I used to wonder
if they were lovers. Then there was only one of them. He
said his friend had died, was taken away by the ambulance
in the middle of the night. I guessed he was taken away at 3
am, for what else could the middle be. Contact tracing had
quarantined their building, but the building was not staying in.

The Beard Video

My friends are growing beards on Instagram as if they are not
afraid of being mistaken for Muslims. They post pictures of
the different stages of their growth. They even post time-lapse
videos as they are working from home. Finally the man whom
I have been stalking since we met at my reading in Kinokuniya
also gets into the act. When I watch his video while lying in
bed, the cotton sheets rattle quietly and pass their thread count
into me, as if I am a curtain of hanging beads easily parted.
My body becomes indistinguishable from the Alice blue bed
sheet. My face is masked efficiently by the pillowslip. To the
facial recognition software and the DNA test, I may as well
not be there. When my boyfriend reports me missing, how will
the building inspector find me? Will he know how to read my
phone dropped by my side of the bed?

The Inauguration Poet

According to the regulations, only eight people are allowed
in the KTV room. A conspiracy of young foreign women
is in attendance. The TV menu presents the following
options: a gunman snipes at the President-elect and kills
him; a gunman snipes at the President-elect and misses
him; the FBI disarms the gunman before he can take up
his position on WhatsApp; the gunman is from the FBI.
A conspiracy of critics takes down the inauguration poet.
They wish to control the narrative. They release a statement
that their target is cancel culture, nothing personal. But who
is the ninth person in the room? After inspecting his nails,
from the left corner he moves to the front, and he sings
'Unchained Melody'.

The Mechanical Dog

The mechanical dog does not wish to be mistaken for a real
dog. Its long-legged purpose is to scare the citizens of this
purpose-built park into wearing their masks. Its eyes, two
video cameras, hunt down offenders tirelessly. Its yellow body
is always on the go. The citizens are, however, unafraid of
the dog. They whisk near to the dog and wish to take selfies
with it. Look, the citizens say, if you abide by the law, what
do you have to be afraid of? The mechanical dog wags its tail
in agreement, activated by the inspector looking through its
eyes. In a distant galaxy, called Shannara or Harlem, the salt
scattered on the icy sidewalk is slowly eating up the concrete.
Munch, munch, what's for lunch?

The Picnic Mat

When they left, the hospital tents in the park had imprinted
neat rectangles of dead grass. A paraphrase of what
happened. A Morse message, all dashes, no dots. Horizontal
smoke signals. QR code. It also reminded me of the AIDS
quilt. Then it was rolled up and put away. The area of possible
infection had been fenced off. The strollers and their nannies
had been careful to keep their distance. The grass had grown
back in a center-left conspiracy. If you again hover in your
helicopter, like an angel on a wire in a Christmas pageant
or a roof inspector, you will say, behold. The picnickers have
returned to their usual spots, with their hampers, books, and
dogs, sitting on the black picnic mats.

The Scout Leader

The search in my underwear is unwarranted. I have not had
a nocturnal emission since I was fifteen, dreaming that my
scout leader was pulling off his shirt and advancing on my
vibrating form. Before he could touch me, I was all wet and
warm below. But now, whenever I write about the dream,
and I am always writing about the dream even when I am
not, the beautiful scout leader wears the air of an inspector
who has a master's degree in detecting signs of child abuse.
His right hand pulses with an ultraviolet light. His left hand
infrared. No matter how hard I write, I cannot change him
back. You know him too. The undeniable UFO that blots out
sun and rain.

The Body Camera

'You cannot bring the body camera with you to the grave,' says the soil inspector. He dips his finger into the batter and tastes it. It is grainy. We are, after all, in the quarterfinals of the Great British Baking Show, where the judgment will be more severe than ever. We are, after all, in the first year of the pandemic. For the technical challenge, Paul and Mary would like you to bake an anti-terrorism sword. It is a Chinese app and everyone will be required to download it onto their phone. You have two-and-a-half hours. You may remove the gingham covering now. The camera is rolling. The anus remembers.

The rat
that leapt off

my back
to enter heaven

first
is still a rat.

I am an ox,
stoic and traditional,

keeping
to the rich furrows

cut by
abiding love.

It's true:
when I was ten

I wished
I were a monkey,

overturning heaven
with my

antics, changing
into a fish,

a freckled bustard,
a roadside

shrine.
But mother died

and went ahead
of me

and all wishes for change
left too.

If I should turn
into

a rooster or a pig,
how would

she recognize her boy
when she

passed by the rocky
fields?

Or, now,
these regions of fire?

THE DREAM CHILD

— so what will Baby/be tomorrow? —
Antonia Pozzi, 'The Dreamed Life'

Who speaks to me speaks
to a stir –
in air, a ripple
of veil – perhaps –
speaking
caused the ripple,
hard to tell.

*

But body is sensed –
joy – as possibility,
everything small
but perfect,
toes,
lips capable
of taking
ravishment – giving.

*

They walk
the woods as others
make love,
the man who
will be sent away
to Rome,

the girl who will lean
back on grass –
trembling
until the slight wind
drops.

*

These children – not theirs –
take up so much space.
They tug, they push.
They stride ahead, expecting the world
to give way.
Even when they tumble,
they cover
ground.

I watch behind the elm
and step out –
a shadow.

*

Only when I open
my throat –
to call, to hiss –
do I
occupy
a place,
as when the sound
of the sea takes up the room
of a shell,
or when sky is skylark.

*

In their rage,
the dead break
things – soup bowls,
flour mills.
I can see
them, foreheads
burning,
but they can't
see – the unborn.

They think they are
looking at a loaf
of fire, water
becoming soup.

*

Whatever else
I am, I am
the earth-clod
on which my parents step
together, her feet
on his feet.

Her fingers weave
between his fingers
like ropes
around a raft.

White wisps –
on a second
look – join

as cloud
and sail off.

I am
left behind.

*

My young mother, my young corpse,
black album
of images – I stroke:
girl graduate,
political meetings,
Alpine flowers,
gay ribbons.

You have baby
photographs.
I – have – nothing.

*

You call me
Herald,
but know me
as entombed waters.

The pen dips
in the waters

and writes its
message of love.

*

To be held
– inside –
your body,

to be fed
by sun

to be cooled
by goodness,

to be born...

to redeem
and be redeemed.

*

Annunzio –
my mother calls in the dark.
I run
towards the name
of my father's
dead brother.

I hear her sweet
urgency
but I can't find her
in the woods.

I run
not with a marguerite
but bayonet.

*

Because my father loves my mother's eyes,
I have her blue eyes.
The more he loves, the more blue.

I have her heart
that beats so fast that I am afraid
it will burst.

At night my sex
opens and opens –
impure lips –
to swallow

the moon.

*

A blessing,
a blessing and – dismissal
of what has already left.

From the interior
of the church –
you see a fountain
shooting up
and toppling,
at a distance too far
to be heard.

The mind has to
provide the music.

PALINODE IN THE VOICE OF MY DEAD FATHER (XII)

There are mysteries
here

that cannot be
described

except
by retraction.

The earth
does not revolve

around
the sun.

The son
does not revolve

around
the father.

PALINODE IN THE VOICE OF MY DEAD FATHER (XIII)

When Stesichorus,
he who fathered

a chorus, retracted
his blaming

Helen for Troy's
devastation,

he recovered
his eyesight.

He could appreciate
beauty again.

Each time I
retract a statement

I made in life,
I recover

my voice.
That's how much

you want the dead
to speak

to you again and again
but only

to contradict
their death,

in other words,
themselves.

THE REPLY

You're silent now, and it's no surprise,
you've been a silent movie all my life.
That's poetry's way of putting it, and it's
dead wrong – you're no Chaplin, funny
and glamorous, although you may be
one of the mini-minions in *Metropolis*.
No, you're not the proof for a thesis.
  My earliest memory is riding on your
shoulders heading home from the merry-
go-round. My last memory, of you living,
your lung walls succumbing to the flooding,
is the speechless and tearless hospital bed,
and me planting a kiss on your forehead.
Between these short clips, you bicycling
down the gentle swerve of road that hugs
the bottom slope of Mount Faber like a rug,
me sitting with my pianica on the top tube,
legs slightly raised to free the circling pedals.
  We're a home movie that nobody wants
to watch, except the family, the ones
knowing, sentimental, and disputatious.
Your four brothers, rich with arrogance,
your two sisters, hard as stale biscuits,
expect you to agree with them, and you do,
backpedalling as you do. There's the rub.
I see it and judge it craven of you,
not seeing then I am your best reply,
what with my school honors and, eventually,
my scholarship to go overseas.
  While mother hogs the weekly phone calls
with talk of winter clothes and shopping malls,

your silence grows and grows on me, profound
as the first snow falling on college grounds.
At the end of time, three long, exciting years,
out of Heathrow mother and you appear
and I'm shocked to see the snow in your hair.
Loveliest of trees, the cherry now
is hung with bloom along the bough...
    To my flowering regret, you've flown the distance
but I deny you the pomp and circumstance.
Thinking myself above empty ceremonies
and you and mother below the Latin service,
I don't sign up for the Sheldonian show,
but throw together an improvised shoot
of us in the college garden, me geared up
and you gamely following this young pup.
Not a word of reproach, not a subtitle,
my Joe pays off his Pip's unpaid bills.
    You won't know the reference, but you
would like Joe, both of you working men,
he a blacksmith and you an electrician,
both of you surviving shits for fathers
with your goodness intact, saving dicks
for sons with your belief in the best of larks.
There I go, showing off my learning
and irreverence, there I go again,
poetrying. I'm still answering my aunts
and dear uncles, who are dying, dead,
or softening to the middle of their heads.
    It's worsening, since living in New York,
I've written book after book after book,
and placed them like bombs in your hands.
You keep them carefully by your bible,
in the high drawer of the TV cabinet,
the cheek by the turn-your-other-cheek.

Where is strength? Where is weakness?
What is truly evil? What is goodness?
The freedom fighter's someone's terrorist,
someone's draft dodger the pacifist.
    This week my XI's read the *Oedipus*
and, like all generations, were nonplussed
by the enormities wrought by right intent,
fleeing father-murder to father-murder,
abjuring mother-sex to sleep with her.
If to save a baby is to kill all babies
through the lightning plague in the city,
what should we do with the mewling
mess, milk-stained, exposed, ankle-torn,
on the green, wooded slopes of Kithairon?
There are some places like Singapore
that would make the careful calculation.
There are some places like Greece, once,
that would pose the question and no more.
You, my father, are the Grecian oracle.
    There I go again. This habit of reading life
as if it's a work of art, this tendency,
grows from the library books devoured
tenderly on the walk home while avoiding
the lances thrusting up like lampposts.
And you encourage me, give me courage –
when at the books corner you leave me
and shop with mother, for life, at OG,
you show me, as an unschooled man's able,
you're replaceable and irreplaceable.
    At your wake, attended by relatives
and a number of poet-friends, I give
the reply of the living to the dead.
For you, looking oddly like bread
in the yellowing husk of your body,

the eulogy begins with the bicycle,
and it says, I remember, I remember.
Just that. All the carefully chosen
phrases reducible to one refrain.

But a letter is not an eulogy – it has
much more of me in it and, at last,
much more of you, my father, in me.
When you're loaded into the oven,
to lift from us the annual burden
of visiting and sweeping your grave,
I'm seized by a wild desire to swear
that before every poetry reading, I'll say,
I'm Koh Jee Leong, the son of Koh Dut Say,
in the manner of the Malays and the Scots.

The desire passes. Let this be the brother,
the guilty brother, to the dead and gone,
the reply a replacement for other ones,
the movie you and I've together caught,
the son you have for the sons you have not.

ACKNOWLEDGEMENTS

Grateful thanks to the editors of these magazines, websites, and anthologies for first publishing some of the poems in this book: *The Abandoned Playground, Eunoia Review, Flypaper Lit, Impossible Archetype, Jogos Florais, Letter to My Father, The Lincoln Review, Lovejets, A Luxury We Cannot Afford, Magma, Manoa, PN Review, Poetry London, Prairie Schooner, The Quarterly Review of Singapore, Queer Southeast Asia, The Rialto, The Sun Isn't Out Long Enough,* and *this/that/lit.*

I am very grateful to the interviewees who shared their stories with me for writing 'A Simple History of Singaporeans in America'.

Andrew Howdle read a draft of this book, and his comments largely shaped the form of the book. Thank you for this and many other kindnesses.

Guy E. Humphrey, my love, I'm so glad that you are in my life. You take me out of my rut.